MW01596469

ANALYSIS

OF

Wintering:

The Power of Rest and Retreat in
Difficult Times

By

Katherine May

AcesPrint

AcesPrint

Copyright (c) 2020

Table of Content

SYNOPSIS:

Wintering (2020) is the compelling account of how author Katherine May learned to embrace a bleak, harsh season in her own life by turning to the lessons of winter. From saunas to cold-winter swimming, wolves to winter solstice, May looks to how animals, plants, and cultures throughout history have survived, and even flourished, in the darkest time of the year.

ABOUT THE AUTHOR:

Katherine May is a writer of both fiction and nonfiction who has a particular fascination with the rhythms of the natural world. Her other books include The Electricity of Every Living Thing and The Whitstable High Tide Swimming Club. She was formerly director of the creative writing program at Canterbury Christ Church University.

DISCLAIMER:

This book is a SUMMARY. It is meant to be a companion, not a replacement, to the original book. Please note that this summary is not authorized, licensed, approved, or endorsed by the author or publisher of the main book. The author of this summary is wholly responsible for the content of this summary and is not associated with the original author or publisher of the main book. If you'd like to purchase the original book, kindly search for the title in the search box.

INTRODUCTION.

What's in it for me? Learn how to winter by observing nature.

Winter is inevitable. It follows autumn just as summer follows spring. In nature, winter is a time of retreat. Under the cover of cold and darkness, plants and animals conserve their energies, rest, and regenerate. Only humans seem to resist winter's call to slow down and regroup.

As inevitable as winter are winter-like periods of life: times that feel bleak and cold and hopeless. Whether it's as a result of illness, bereavement, job loss, or heartbreak, each of us will weather our own personal winters.

Learning to embrace the season can offer strategies for coping in life's darker times. When we connect our own struggles with the rhythms of the natural world, we tap into profound and time-tested strategies for surviving until spring.

In these chapters, you'll learn

- why it's essential to prepare for winter periods;
- how cold-water swimming can open us up to winter's joys; and
- What ants and bees can teach us about surviving winter.

Like winter, challenging periods of life are natural and inevitable.

A week before her 40th birthday, the author, Katherine May, was gathered with friends on a beach in Folkestone, when her husband complained of feeling ill. At first, they were both inclined to dismiss it as a minor ailment, but over the course of the day he grew steadily worse.

By the evening he was admitted to the emergency ward with what he suspected was appendicitis. Treatment was deferred until the following morning, and in the night his appendix burst. For a week his life hung in the balance. His recovery was equally slow and painful.

For the author, this was just the beginning of a fraught and challenging season in her life.

The key message is: Like winter, challenging periods of life are natural and inevitable.

At the time her husband fell ill, May's life was already in flux. She'd just given notice at her academic job and was hoping to find fulfillment outside the nine-to-five. Shortly after her husband's illness, she began to notice signs of ill health in herself. After months of increasingly debilitating symptoms and grueling tests, she was diagnosed with Crohn's disease, a type of inflammatory bowel disorder. No longer a productive employee, she suddenly found herself unemployed and unable to do the creative work she'd envisioned.

The author's son was also in distress. Just six, he already felt pressure to meet academic targets at school and was traumatized by the bullying of his peers. So the author made the difficult decision to embark on homeschooling.

Illness, upheaval, and anguish forced May out of her routine. She rested. She slowed down. She allowed herself to feel sad. She paid more attention to the world around her. She even began to find pleasure in this new way of living.

She'd always been interested in the natural world and its rhythms. And so, in a period of her life that felt as bleak and harsh as winter, she began to look to that season for lessons. She noticed that, unlike humans, plants and animals don't try to resist winter. They know that winter is very different from summer. So they adapt or hibernate. They gather their resources, rest, and regenerate. When the season has passed, they emerge, transformed.

She began to think that wintering might be as essential to humans as it is to plants and other animals.

When you see winter coming, begin to prepare

There's a Finnish word, talvitelat, that has no direct English translation, and refers to the preparations Finns make ahead of winter. Winter arrives hard and fast in Finland, and the season can be long and hard: it pays to be prepared. So Finns begin to ready themselves at the very first hint of frost. They store their summer clothes and unpack their sweater stash and snow boots. They chop and stack firewood. They buy winter tires for their cars and make sure the roofs of their houses are in good enough repair to withstand the weight of heavy snowfall.

Sometimes, these preparations can begin as early as August, when summer is in full swing.

Here's the key message: When you see winter coming, begin to prepare.

If you don't live somewhere like Finland, where the winters are extreme, the idea of preparing for the season may strike you as less urgent. But even in milder climes, talvitelat can bring its own benefits.

Beginning in the autumn, make your own preparations. This could mean baking bread and cakes to store in the freezer, gathering candles and fairy lights to bring warmth into your home, or pickling and preserving the last of the summer's fruits and vegetables.

Note that stocking up your kitchen doesn't mean making a bulk order on Amazon. The point is to engage in the kind of slow, mindful work that creates space for reflection. Work like kneading dough or untangling fairy lights.

This kind of thoughtful toil can also bring seasonality back into everyday life. These days, our working lives – and, by consequence, our periods of leisure – can feel seasonless. There are no ebbs and flows to the rhythm of contemporary work. We're expected to produce at a grueling, constant pace, and stay logged-on even during our off hours. These slow activities can become a moving meditation that signals a time of slowing down and rest.

Take note, though. Preparing for winter shouldn't mean pushing the cold away. Cold has healing properties: think of ice, applied to a burn. The Finns, who prepare so assiduously for winter, still embrace it. A popular winter tradition is to follow a steaming sauna with a naked roll in the snow or a jump in a frozen lake.

The point of your preparations isn't to avoid winter, but to gather the resources to face it.

Winter is a time for rest and contemplation.

For humans, the cold and the dark have become nuisances. We resist them with thermal clothes, indoor heating, electric lights, and glowing screens.

Animals like dormice, on the other hand, hibernate through the winter months in nests made from moss and bark. Other animals, like badgers and frogs, don't hibernate for lengthy periods but reach a state of torpor on cold days, where they drop their body temperatures and slow their heart rates.

For these animals, cold dark weather isn't a nuisance but a signal to rest. Perhaps we should begin looking at it the same way.

This is the key message: Winter is a time for rest and contemplation.

Winter is an invitation to sleep longer. Cold temperatures make early nights under blankets seem tempting and dark mornings create perfect conditions for sleeping in. All too often, we resist the call to rest. Thanks to electric lights and LED alarm clocks bookending the dark with artificial light, there's no need to change our sleeping patterns in winter.

But it wasn't always like this.

Before the Industrial Revolution, observes historian A. Roger Ekirch, on long, dark nights, we slept in shifts. We went to bed at sunset but would rise in the early hours of the morning for the watch, a time to visit the bathroom, or smoke, but also to talk, pray, and reflect. Following the watch, we'd sleep until daybreak.

And it seems this long sleep, with a period of wakefulness, might be both hardwired into us and beneficial for our health. When a 1996 study attempted to replicate the conditions of winter sleep in prehistoric times, participants were deprived of light for 14 hours a night. After a few days, they began to naturally wake up to perform a watch of sorts. Fascinatingly, in this time, they were observed to be calm and reflective.

What do we lose by rejecting our ancestral sleep habits and resisting winter's call to sleep longer? Rest, certainly. But perhaps we also lose the chance to linger in our dreams, to sit with the anxieties that wake us in a panic and let them pass by, or the chance to explore the meditative state between sleeping and wakefulness that is possible during long periods of rest.

Rituals create solidarity and community in dark times.

In the secular, Western calendar, what milestones mark the year? Christmas, whether or not you celebrate the holiday's religious aspects, is widely observed along with New Year's Eve. Most people expect to take a week or two of summer vacation, too. And then? Well, that's about it.

Compare this to the Druidic calendar, patterned after the Wheel of the Year. Every six weeks, druids observe a ritual connected with the passing of time and the season. Imbolc is observed at the start of February to mark the beginning of spring. It's followed by Alban Eilir, the spring equinox, and Beltane, or May Day.

In the depths of winter, druids observe Alban Arthan, the winter equinox. This is the shortest day and the longest night of the year. And they're not alone in this.

The key message here is: Rituals create solidarity and community in dark times.

Throughout history, across cultures and religions, the winter solstice has coincided with important festivals. In Scandinavian regions, for example, St. Lucy's day is widely celebrated in mid-December. One story told is that as a young girl in Rome, Lucy visited persecuted Christians hiding in the city's catacombs, wearing a crown of candles to light her way. In present-day St. Lucy rituals, girls wear similar crowns – connecting with the story of the original Lucy and also symbolizing the gradual transition from darkness to light that begins on the solstice.

Whether it's St. Lucy's Day, Alban Arthan, or Christmas, there's something especially potent about the rituals which occur around the time of the winter solstice. But any form of ritual connected to the calendar makes welcome space for us both to measure the passing of time and to pause and reflect. While summertime rituals are focused on celebration and festivity, those in wintertime are often focused on community and solidarity – recognizing that winter is a hard and brutal time. If we're to come through it, we need to pull together and find ways to light up the dark.

You don't need to be a druid, or even religious, to partake in wintertime rituals. Sometimes, the most potent are the ones you invent for yourself. You can find community in nature, making a ritual of long winter walks in now-empty landscapes. Or perhaps through time with friends and family, doing something as simple as hosting a regular wintertime dinner gathering, where everyone cooks and eats together. The key thing is to cultivate connection with the world, ensuring you don't observe the darkest moments of the year alone.

Wolves are unfairly typecast as wintery villains.

In popular culture, wolves are often associated with winter – and this association is far from positive. Think of literature. In C. S. Lewis's Narnia books, for example, wolves are the evil foot soldiers of the White Witch, whose sinister magic has left the land of Narnia frozen in permanent winter. George R. R. Martin's A Song of Ice and Fire books open with the appearance of five dire wolf pups. As they grow, the pups become omens of an approaching, cataclysmic Winter which threatens to devastate the land.

In contemporary Europe, you're far more likely to encounter a fictional wolf than a real one. But this wasn't always the case.

Here's the key message: Wolves are unfairly typecast as wintery villains.

Currently, the global wolf population stands at around 300,000. Twelve thousand of these are estimated to roam Europe. But in the pre-industrial age, wolves were widespread across both the United Kingdom and the continent. In Anglo-Saxon England, the first full moon of January was known as the Wolf Moon. This was the time when, driven by hunger and a lack of available prey, wolves left the forest in packs to hunt villagers' livestock.

As a species, they were widely despised for this practice. Wolf-hunting was a common medieval winter activity. Tenants could even pay rent by delivering wolfskins to their landlords. Criminals were often asked to pay their fines with severed wolf tongues. Eventually, this antagonism was sanctioned by the monarchy. In 1272, King Edward decreed that wolves should be exterminated from England. By 1509, they were all but extinct.

Still, they remain wintertime symbols of meanness and hunger. But the stereotype of the savage wolf is incorrect. Wolves live and travel in extremely devoted family packs. They're loving partners and parents. Typically, they're only driven to eat livestock in times of extreme scarcity.

So, what is it about wolves that scares us? Naturalist Barry Lopez observes that wolves have a feast-or-famine mentality. For this reason, they're one of only two animals that kill and consume more than they need; they're always looking ahead to the next lean time.

The other animal? Humans. We consume far more than we need to survive. We're convinced that spending money will satiate our desires, and when it doesn't, we spend more. Our impact on our environment has been nothing short of disastrous.

Perhaps our loathing of wolves stems from the fact that we see our own worst appetites reflected in them. Instead of spending winter being scared of wolves, whether literal or metaphorical, we could spend this time confronting our own wolfish natures.

Extreme weather and temperatures can bring out the best in us.

Snow, while beautiful, is seen by many as an inconvenience. When it accumulates – a less and less frequent occurrence in many parts of the world – it crashes the whole system. In a world where almost everything can be seamlessly managed with the click of a mouse or the swipe of a card, it's humbling to see how the weather can still bring us to a standstill.

Heavy snow can make roads impassable, stop trains in their tracks, and isolate villages from the outside world. But snow also beckons even serious adults to reconnect with a playful side of their nature – perhaps because it forces us to slow down and pay more attention to our surroundings. There's something about snow that tempts even grown-ups to trace out a snow angel on the ground or make a dapper snowman.

The key message is: Extreme weather and temperatures can bring out the best in us.

Like snow, the extreme cold of a winter sea or lake has something to teach us about slowing down. Many of us regard swimming in the sea and splashing in lakes as summertime activities. In winter, the icy cold of the same water we enjoyed in summer drives us away. But while cold-water swimming is a different experience, it's no less valuable.

There are documented physiological advantages to cold-water swimming. Immersion in cold water leads to a roughly 25 -percent increase in dopamine, the neurotransmitter which stimulates the brain's pleasure centers. And a 2000 study found that cold-water swimming measurably decreases tension and fatigue and lifts mood.

There are less easily documented benefits, too. Cold-water swimmers report feeling intensely present while they're swimming. In the water, their past regrets and anxieties about the future drift away; the extreme temperature means they're forced to focus on the moment, paying attention only to the effects of the cold on their bodies. In this sense, cold-water swimming requires mindfulness. It also cultivates resilience – the act in itself is an innately resilient one. So, regular cold-water swims shore up our belief in our own capacity for resilience.

Slowness, playfulness, mindfulness, resilience: far from being inconvenient, the extremes of winter weather are a gift that allows us to reconnect with these qualities in ourselves.

Winter fosters community.

In one of his famous fables, Aesop, the ancient Greek storyteller, recounts the tale of the ant and the grasshopper. The grasshopper enjoys the summer months and enjoys the lazy, sunny days. The ant, meanwhile, spends the summertime industriously gathering grains of wheat for winter.

When leaner months arrive, the grasshopper has nothing to eat. Desperate, the grasshopper asks the ant to share its harvest, but the ant scoffs: the grasshopper didn't do enough work during the summer, so it doesn't deserve to survive the winter.

This is the key message: Winter fosters community.

Aesop clearly means for us to emulate the well-prepared ant, but, in truth, this is a cruel story. During some seasons in our lives, we'll behave more like the grasshopper than the ant, reveling in pleasure and letting harder times catch us unprepared. Other times, much as we might like to save, we'll simply have no grains to gather.

But, while recognizing that we have a grasshopper side to our natures, we can still learn from the ant. Ants work in harmony, each contributing to the greater good of the colony. Honeybees do the same.

Honeybees are most visible in summer as they collect nectar from flowers. But the bulk of their work lies in preparing for winter which they'll spend, from October to April, in their hives. The nectar they collect is mixed with an enzyme that naturally occurs in their stomachs, and is stored as honey in the hive's honeycomb. Should a bee return to the hive with a belly full of nectar and find there are no vacant cells in the comb, a chemical reaction causes the nectar to turn into wax, which is used for building the next cell.

With enough honey stashed to last the winter, the honeybees now need to stay warm. They do this by detaching their wings from their flight muscles, huddling together, and working those muscles to raise their body temperatures. When the heater bees at the center grow tired, new bees take over. In this way, even on bitter winter days, the cold-blooded bees can maintain a temperature of 35 degrees Celsius in the hive.

The sociobiologist E. O. Wilson classifies bees and ants as eusocial creatures, which cooperate in service of a common goal. Wilson believes humans are also innately eusocial, although complex political and economic factors may cause us to forget this.

The real lesson we can learn from our fellow eusocial creatures? Working together, we can all survive lean winter seasons.

Nature teaches us how to endure our personal winters.

After her study of winter in the natural world, and learning how various cultures and species have adapted to it, the author embraced a new approach to dealing with dark and challenging personal times.

In the wake of illness, career change, and family upheaval, she learned to apply the lessons of the season to her own life. In essence, she learned "wintering."

Here's the key message: Nature teaches us how to endure our personal winters.

Here are some of the lessons the author believes we should embrace.

To begin with, human life, like all natural life, comes in seasons. But we're encouraged to deny this simple fact and urged to put a positive spin on even the worst life experiences. In short, we're programmed to resist winter and act as if our lives are one long, continuous summer.

Across social media, we're bombarded with inspirational quotes, encouraging relentless, even toxic, positivity. Society's focus is on finding ways to survive and thrive in the face of challenges. The message? We must cope with our difficulties whatever the cost.

But, over the course of a harvest cycle, fields must spend one season lying fallow, lest their resources be exhausted and their fertility lost. Just like fields, we too need to lie fallow. Our winters should be a time to hunker down, strip back to the basics, and focus on our own well-being and survival.

Just like the season, our personal winters aren't something to be overcome once and forgotten. They're cyclical, endlessly returning. To someone in the depths of a particularly hard winter, this may be hard to hear. But there's good news, too. Wintering is an acquired skill: each time you do it, you become better prepared for the next.

With practice, you'll learn to see winter coming and prepare. Your body and your rhythms will begin, automatically, to slow down. You'll learn to cultivate the quieter pleasures of this season. You might even learn how to embrace it. Just as going on a long winter walk or plunging into the frigid ocean can open you up to the thrill of winter, embracing your fallow periods can open you up to their restorative gifts.

Remember, just because winter has unique challenges to overcome doesn't lessen its unique joys. And at times when your winter feels too much to bear, remember that the hard work of winter is preparing you for the rebirth of spring.

FINAL SUMMARY:

The key message in these summary:

Many of us have organized our lives to avoid winter: we resist both the pleasures and challenges of the season and try to push through personal winter periods. But just as giving in to the season offers us the chance to rest and regenerate, embracing the challenges of our personal winters allows us to emerge transformed when they come to a close.

Actionable advice:

Find the color in winter.

Winter has a reputation as a bleak and depressing season, compared to the colorful joys of spring and summer and the mellow tones of autumn. But winter isn't entirely colorless. The absence of green leaves and pastel blossoms can reveal silvery skies, bright red berries, and orange fox fur. Stay alert to the season's unique shades and specific beauty.

Made in the USA
Middletown, DE
27 January 2022

59826472R00024